Art & Activities for Kids

Paint!

Kim Solga

NORTH
LIGHT
BOOKS

Cincinnati, Ohio

Note to Parents and Teachers

The activities in this book were developed for the enjoyment of children. We've taken every precaution to ensure their safety and success. Please follow the directions, and note where an adult's help is required. In fact, feel free to work alongside your young artists as often as you can. They will appreciate help in reading and learning new techniques, and will love the chance to talk and show off their creations. Children thrive on attention and praise, and art adventures are the perfect setting for both.

Quality printing and binding arranged by Regent Publishing Services, Ltd.

98 97 96   7 6 5

Library of Congress Cataloging in Publication Data

Solga, Kim.
  Paint! / Kim Solga.
    p. cm.
  Summary: Presents step-by-step instructions for producing artwork using paint and other materials usually found around the house.
  ISBN 0-89134-383-0
  1. Children as artists—Juvenile literature. 2. Project method in teaching—Juvenile literature.   [1. Painting—Technique.]
I. Title.
N351.S6   1991
702'.8—dc20   90-28434
                                                CIP
                                                AC

Edited by Julie Wesling Whaley
Designed by Clare Finney
Photography Direction by Kristi Kane Cullen
Art Production by Suzanne Whitaker
Photography by Pamela Monfort
Very special thanks to Niki Smith, Nicole Dorst, Lara Muehlenbach and Alison Wenstrup

About This Book (A Note to Grown-Ups)

Paint! features eleven unique painting projects plus numerous variations that will fire the imagination of boys and girls aged six to eleven. By inviting kids to try new things, *Paint!* encourages individual creativity. Young artists will love "breaking the rules" of painting even while they're learning important principles of art. Rather than painting only with brushes, they'll be using craft sticks, cotton-tip swabs, fingers, marbles, and brushes they make themselves out of cotton and feathers—even balloons! They'll learn to make their own paints out of egg yolks and vegetable oil with ground chalk or powdered drink mix for pigments. Not limited to paper, they'll paint on cloth, foil, rocks, faces—even windows—all the while learning about blending colors, paint texture, translucency, proportion and much more.

Each project has a theme, stated at the very beginning, and some projects suggest follow-up activities related to that theme. Some projects result in beautiful finished works to display or give away; others emphasize experimentation and the simple fun of *doing* them. They're all kid-tested to ensure a high success rate and inspire confidence.

Getting the Most Out of the Projects

Each project is both fun to do and educational. While the projects provide clear step-by-step instructions and photographs, each is open-ended so kids may decide what *they* want to paint. Some of the projects are easy to do in a short amount of time. Others require more patience and even adult supervision. The symbols on page 6 will help you recognize the more challenging activities.

The list of materials shown at the beginning of each activity is for the featured project only. Suggested alternatives may require different supplies. Feel free to substitute! For example, Pudding Paint recreates the thick texture of undiluted acrylic paint straight from the tube. If cooking up a batch of paint isn't for you, your child could do the activity with non-toxic acrylics, though this is a more expensive alternative. The projects offer flexibility to make it easy for you and your child to try as many activities as you wish.

Collecting Supplies

All of the projects can be done with household items or inexpensive, easy-to-find supplies (see page 7 for definitions of any art materials you're not already familiar with). Here are some household items you'll want to make sure you have on hand: newspapers, paper plates, muffin tins or egg cartons (for holding and mixing different colors of paint), scrap paper, scrap cardboard, cotton swabs, squeeze bottle (from mustard or dish soap, for example), magazines (for photos and ideas), foil, plastic wrap, waxed paper, white glue, flour, salt, sugar, breakfast cereal, marbles, liquid laundry starch, white cloth and scrap cloth, sponges.

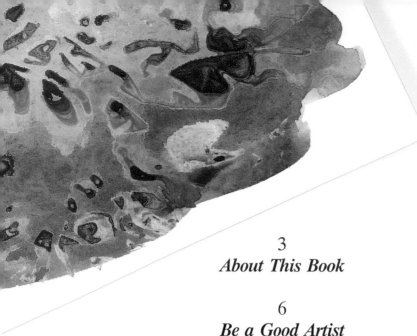

Be a Good Artist

Work Habits

Get permission to work at your chosen workspace before you begin. Cover your workspace with newspapers or a vinyl tablecloth.

Wear a smock or big, old T-shirt to protect your clothes.

Follow the directions carefully for each project. When you see this symbol, have an adult help you.

Don't put art materials in your mouth. If you're working with a younger child, don't let him put art materials in his mouth, either.

The clock symbol means you must wait to let something dry before going on to the next step. It is very important not to rush ahead.

Finish by cleaning your workspace and all of your tools. Wash brushes in warm water until the water runs clear, and store with bristles up.

Collecting Supplies

Most of the supplies you'll need for each project can be found around the house. You'll want to collect them for your art projects.

You will want to keep a few paper plates and egg cartons to mix paint in. Plastic margarine tubs are great for rinse water.

Save old squeeze bottles and sponges. Look for unused white cloth and scrap cloth, old magazines and newspapers.

Art Terms

Tempera paint. Also called poster paint, tempera paint is a water-based paint that is opaque—you can't see through it. You buy it at an art supply store already mixed with water (a liquid paint in a bottle or jar) or as a powder that you mix yourself with an adult's help.

Watercolor paint. A water-based paint that is transparent—you can see through it when you paint with it. It comes in little trays of dry paint that you get wet with a paintbrush and water.

Acrylic paint. A water-based plastic paint that's thick and shiny. It comes in a tube or squeeze bottle. You mix it with water to paint, but it's permanent once it's dry.

Paintbrushes. There are many different kinds of brushes. You may want to buy several, from fine-point watercolor brushes to square, heavy-bristle brushes. It's fun to paint with big brushes from the hardware store, too!

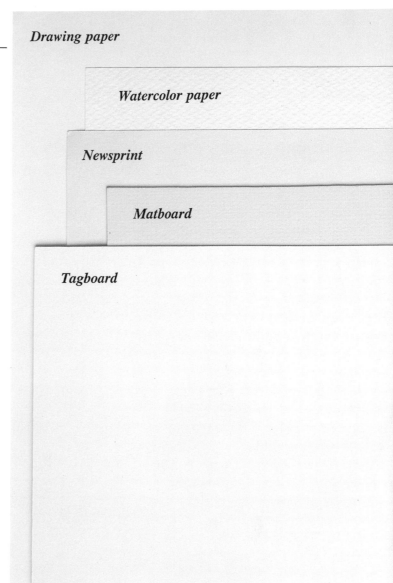

Drawing paper
Watercolor paper
Newsprint
Matboard
Tagboard

Drawing paper. Any white paper, like writing paper, or something heavier like construction paper.

Watercolor paper. Heavy, white or off-white paper with a bumpy surface. You can buy it wherever art supplies are sold.

Newsprint. Gray paper that newspapers are printed on. This paper costs less than good, white paper like watercolor paper. Newsprint is available in rolls for big paintings (you can buy it at an art supply store, or ask any newspaper office for a "roll end").

Matboard. Fancy cardboard that goes around a picture inside a frame. It comes in all colors at framing stores (ask for scraps) or art supply stores.

Tagboard. Also called poster board, tagboard is thinner than matboard. You can buy it wherever school supplies are sold.

Crystal Colors

Color Blending

Have you ever found the windows covered with lacy frost on a cold, winter morning? Was it Jack Frost who painted the delicate designs, or simply water molecules freezing into crystal formations? This watercolor project captures the beautiful look of frost crystals in an explosion of color.

Materials needed:

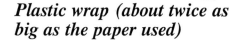

Plastic wrap (about twice as big as the paper used)

Watercolors

Rinse water

Fat watercolor brushes

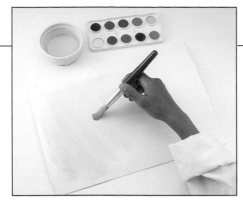

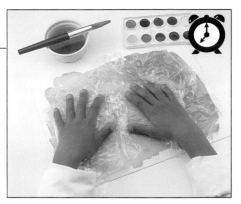

1 "Paint" clear water onto your paper. Then paint big patches of bright colors on the wet paper. Let the colors spread out and blend.

2 If you wish, drip and splatter on your color patches, but work quickly to cover your paper with pools of bright colors.

3 Crumple a big piece of plastic wrap and pat it gently down on top of your wet painting. Set it in a safe place to dry overnight.

White drawing paper or
watercolor paper

Crystal Textures

When you pull the plastic off your dry painting, you'll be amazed at the texture left behind! You can get wonderful colors and patterns with colored ink, tempera paint and acrylics. Try pressing other materials onto wet paint. Experiment with as many different textures as you can!

Aluminum Foil

Waxed Paper

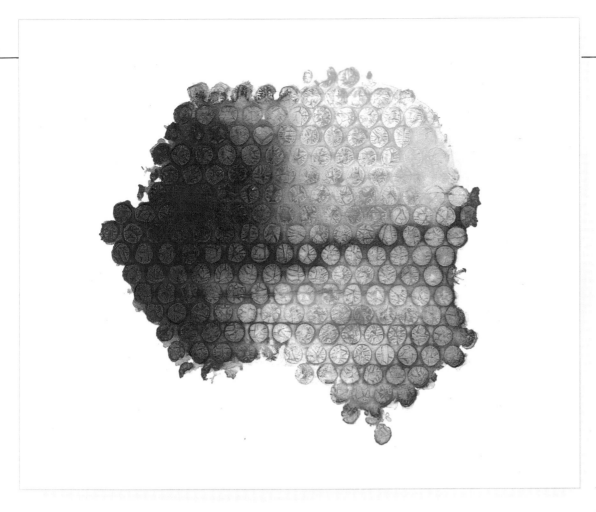

Bubble Wrap

***Leaves and
Flowers***

11

Pudding Paint

Mastering Texture

Pudding Paint looks a lot like ketchup, mustard and mayonnaise, with some blueberry and chocolate pudding on the side. Not much of a snack, but you sure can have fun with this thick paint, cooked like pudding and spread on cardboard with craft sticks.

Pudding paint recipe: (Ask an adult to help you.) Mix 5 cups water, 2 cups white flour, ½ cup sugar, and 3 tablespoons salt. Pour into a saucepan and cook over medium heat until thick and bubbling (about 7 minutes). Cool well. This can be stored in the refrigerator in covered containers for several weeks.

Pudding paint mixture

Materials needed:

Craft sticks and a spoon

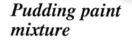

Tempera paint (powdered or liquid)

2 paper plates and 5 containers for mixing

1 Spoon cooled "pudding" into 5 containers and mix with ⅛- to ¼-cup powdered or liquid tempera paint to make 5 main colors.

2 Place spoonfuls of the main colors on one paper plate; use another plate to mix colors. Use craft sticks to paint on cardboard.

3 Pull up to get pointy peaks, or scrape a design into the paint. Make an abstract design, or paint a realistic picture.

Cardboard, tagboard or matboard (the heavier the better)

13

Recipes for Fun

Starchy Paint

Mix powdered tempera paint with liquid laundry starch.
Add just enough starch to make a thick, shiny paint. Work
with stiff brushes on cardboard.

Sawdust Paint

Add spoonfuls of sawdust or crushed breakfast cereal to any liquid paint for a grainy, bumpy texture.

Salt Paint

Stir regular table salt into liquid tempera for a thick, sandy paint. The mixture creates interesting textures as it dries.

Dots of Color

Exploring Pointillism

Painting a picture with dots instead of lines gives your work an extra special look. Here's a project that uses bright paint and cotton-tip swabs. Remember—paint only dots and dots and more dots!

Materials needed:

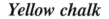
Yellow chalk

Tempera paint

Cotton-tip swabs

Paint tray

White drawing paper

1 Sketch your picture lightly with yellow chalk. The faint lines will brush off easily when your painting is dry.

2 Outline the main shapes of your picture with cotton-tip swabs dipped in paint. Use a new swab for each color.

3 Fill in the shapes with more dots. For smaller dots, pull the cotton away and use just the cardboard stick.

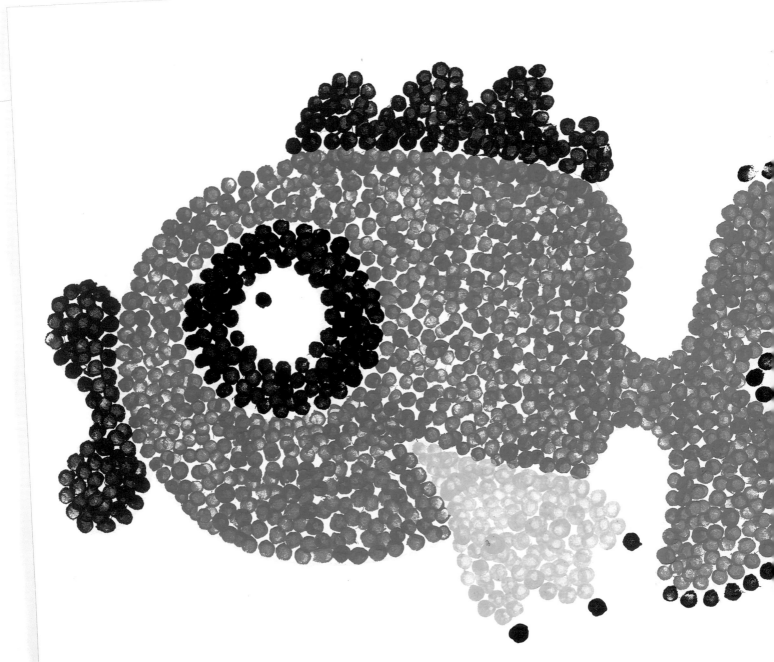

Lots of Dots

Lots of subjects make great Dots of Color paintings! Even small objects you can trace look special when you fill in the familiar shapes with colored dots.

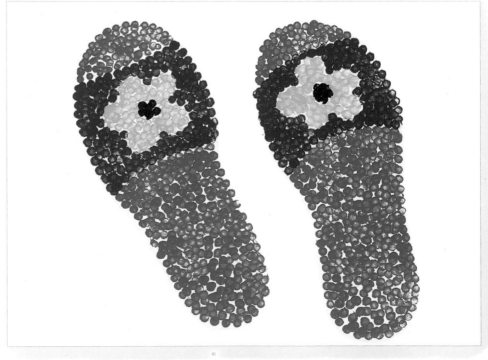

When you look at a picture printed in a magazine or newspaper, you see what appear to be solid colors. But they're actually dots of color! Look closely at the comics in the Sunday newspaper and you'll see it's true.

Stained Glass

Understanding Translucency

Have you ever seen stained glass windows in a church or old house? They're beautiful because they're *translucent*—they allow light to shine through. You can create a "stained glass" window in your home, with special paints you mix yourself.

Materials needed:

Paintbrushes

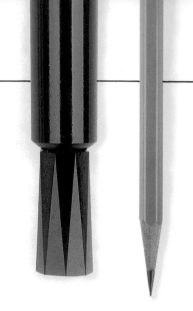

Spoon

Pencil and a black marker

Tempera paint, water, liquid dish soap, and containers

Plastic squeeze bottle

1 Get permission to decorate a sunny window in your home. Cover the windowsill, floor, and the walls with newspaper.

2 Draw a stained glass design on paper first. Sketch a pattern or simple picture, leaving lots of open spaces for different colors.

3 Make your pencil lines dark or use a black marker. Tape your sketch to the outside of the window, with your design facing in.

Masking tape

Drawing paper and newspaper

4 You'll need black paint as thick as mayonnaise. Mix liquid tempera paint with cornstarch or flour if it needs thickening.

5 Spoon the thick black paint into the squeeze bottle. It will be easier to squeeze the paint out if the bottle is full.

6 Squeeze black paint on the inside of the window along the outline of your design. Let it dry for two hours.

Glass Art

Suncatcher

Make a suncatcher on a piece of acrylic (available at window and plate glass shops) or glass in an old picture frame. Follow these same directions. Then, when it's dry, attach a wire or small chain to the picture frame and hang it from a small nail in the frame of a sunny window.

7 Mix several colors of tempera paint with water and a bit of dish soap. The mixed paints should be runny like syrup.

8 When the black paint is all dry, use regular paintbrushes to paint your translucent colors into the spaces of your design.

9 Your stained glass painting can be cleaned off later with soap and water. You may have to scrape to get the black paint off.

Build a Better Brush

Art Has No Rules

What if you went on a camping trip to do some artwork, far away from any town, and you packed all your paints and paper but forgot your paintbrushes—what would you do? You'd have to invent your own! Here are some examples of handmade brushes. Try making them yourself, or create your own, and use them when you paint pictures.

The Balloon Brush
Tie four or five small balloons onto a stick with wire. Use them as they are or cut them into strips.

The Straw Brush
Make a stiff brush by tying together pieces of hay or straw—or pine needles—and attaching them to a stick.

The Housepet Brush
Gather a small handful of your dog's or cat's hair, bunch it together, and tie it onto a stick.

The Feather Brush
Paint a picture with a bunch of feathers held together with a twist of wire.

Bark Brushes
A piece of soft bark that is partially frayed apart makes a great brush.

Ready-Made Brushes
Some dry weeds make interesting brushes just the way they are. Try painting with a stalk of broccoli!

The Cotton Puff Brush
Secure a cotton ball to the end of a stick with a twist of wire.

25

Marble Rolling

Appreciating Abstract Design

Make beautiful rainbow-colored confetti paintings by rolling painted marbles (or beads or ten-
nis balls) on paper taped in a box lid. It's so
much fun, you won't want to stop!

Materials needed:

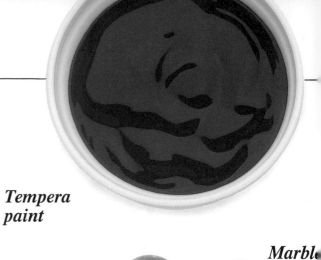

*Tempera
paint*

Marble

Spoon and small dishes

Box lid

1 Pour paint into dishes and drop two or three marbles into each color. Lift them out and set them on paper taped in the box lid.

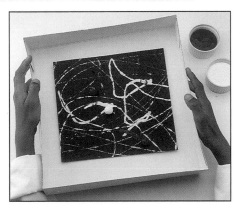

2 Tip the box lid so the marbles roll around. When the paint is used up, dunk the marbles back into the paint—add new colors.

3 Try taping a smaller piece of paper in the middle of the larger one. When you lift it off, you'll see a white design left behind!

Face Painting

Painting Expressions

The artist becomes the art! Learn how to paint happy and sad, ferocious and curious—right on your own face. Painting expressions is an important part of making faces look realistic.

Materials needed:

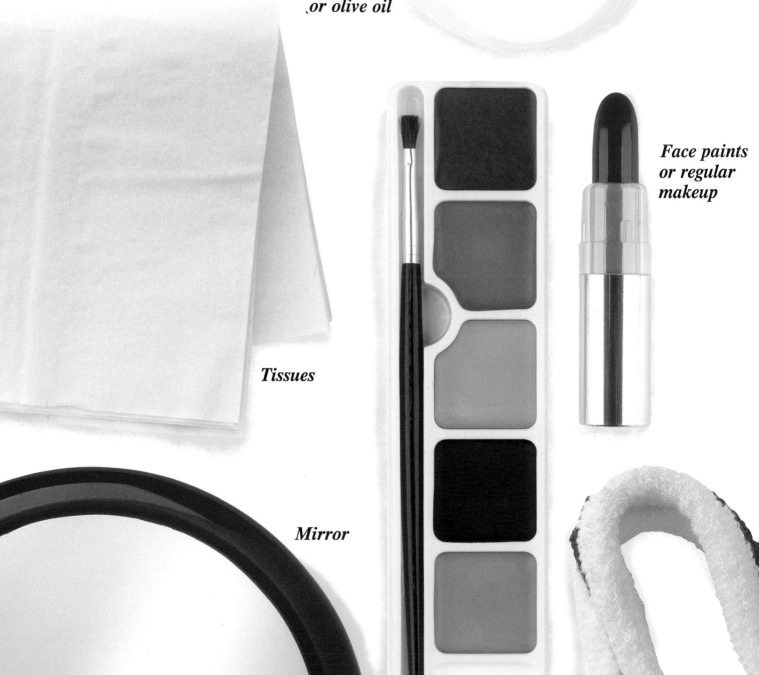

Towel

Cold cream or olive oil

Face paints or regular makeup

Tissues

Mirror

Sponge pieces

Paintbrush

Headband

1 Hold your hair back with a headband and cover your clothes with a towel.

2 Rub cold cream or olive oil on your skin before using regular makeup.

3 Use your fingers or a small piece of sponge to spread paint on your skin.

4 Never get close to your eyes with oil, makeup or paint. Use a paintbrush to make fine lines.

Makeup is easier to remove if you rub most of it off with cold cream or olive oil and tissues first, then wash with warm water and soap.

29

People Faces

Professional clowns begin with white and then add darker colors one by one. You should paint your face this way, too. Be careful not to smear colors together.

Happy Clown

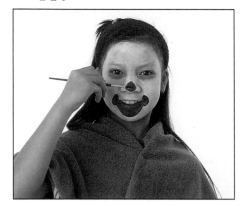

1 Paint your face white. Make a bright red smile and a red nose.

2 Add red freckles. Use black to make high, half-moon eyebrows and little sparkle lines by your eyes.

Sad "Hobo" Clown

3 Paint a gray patch around your mouth. Paint a red nose and a big red frown. Darken your eyebrows and add a teardrop.

Monster

Zany Face

4 Make a scar! Spread a thin line of *nontoxic* white glue on one cheek. Pinch your skin together as the glue dries. Paint your whole face pale green.

5 Make dark gray shadows around your eyes and dark lines down from your nose to your chin. A touch of red on the fake scar adds a ghastly effect.

6 Cover your eyebrows with white triangles and paint long black eyelash lines. Make red lips with dots at each side of your mouth. Add lightning bolts to your cheeks.

Animal Faces

Shy Raccoon

Make a basic snout—paint your cheeks white before painting the whiskers on. Make a black raccoon mask around your eyes. Color your forehead and the sides of your face gray or brown.

Basic Snout

1 Make a white patch around your mouth. Use a paintbrush to draw a black or brown line down each side of your nose.

2 Paint the tip of your nose black. Make a black line under your nose down to the middle of your upper lip.

3 Extend the line both ways along your lip and curve it up. Paint a few dots on your upper lip and draw long whiskers onto your cheeks.

Design your own animal face. Look at a photograph of the animal and use some of the ideas here (it's fun to practice on dolls).

Ferocious Tiger
Make a basic snout without the whiskers. Paint white around your eyes. Color the rest of your face orange. Paint black stripes on your forehead and cheeks, and white fangs on your lower lip.

Friendly Panda
Make a basic snout but leave the whiskers off and don't paint the lines along your nose. Paint your cheeks and forehead white. Make big black patches around your eyes down onto your cheeks.

Curious Monkey
Paint white in kind of a heart shape up over your eyes and around your face. Color your forehead and the sides of your face brown. Outline your nose, nostrils, and mouth with black and make dark eyebrows.

Shine On

Experimenting with Media

Create a painting that sparkles without using paint or paper. "Paint" with tissue paper and glue onto aluminum foil for a picture so shiny and bright you'll need sunglasses to look at it!

Materials needed:

Wide paintbrush

Mixing dish and water

White glue

Shiny stickers (or sequins)

Glitter

Metallic thread

1 Mix equal amounts of glue and water. It looks milky white but will dry clear and shiny.

2 Spread out a piece of foil, shiny side up. Tear colored tissue paper into strips and pieces. Brush some glue mixture onto the foil.

3 Lay a piece of tissue paper down, then brush more glue over it. Keep adding tissue and glue, overlapping the tissue pieces to make a design.

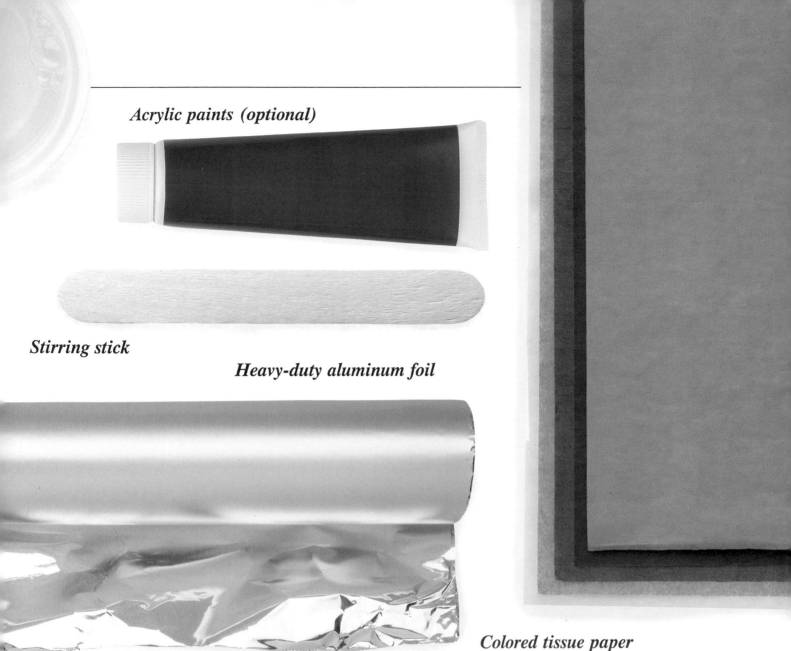

Acrylic paints (optional)

Stirring stick

Heavy-duty aluminum foil

Colored tissue paper

4 The tissue paper soaks up the wet glue and becomes your "paint." Create new colors where the tissue overlaps—even the glue turns colors.

5 Add shiny stickers, sequins, and metallic thread to make your painting sparkle. Use acrylic paints if you want some darker areas in your design.

6 Sprinkle glitter on top of your wet painting for a shimmery effect. When you're all finished, let your painting dry overnight.

Shiny Fun

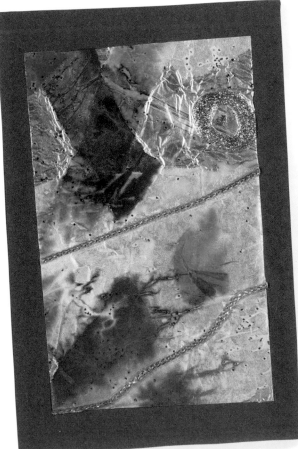

Paint a picture or abstract design. Wrap the foil around sturdy cardboard to make a poster. Or cut small sections out of a big foil design and glue them onto folded construction paper to make shiny greeting cards.

Wrap your foil painting around a can to make a beautiful pencil holder or flower pot. Or use your sparkle painting to wrap a present—it's perfect for gifts you bake or make yourself.

Half and Half Paintings

Measuring Proportions

This project is a partnership between you and a photographer. Half of the picture is made up of photos cut out of a magazine, then you paint the other half. Try painting half a person or cartoon character. Or try using a black-and-white photo, mixing different shades of gray to match.

Materials needed:

Tempera paints and paintbrush

Pencil

Scissors

Old magazines

Heavy drawing paper and scrap paper

Glue

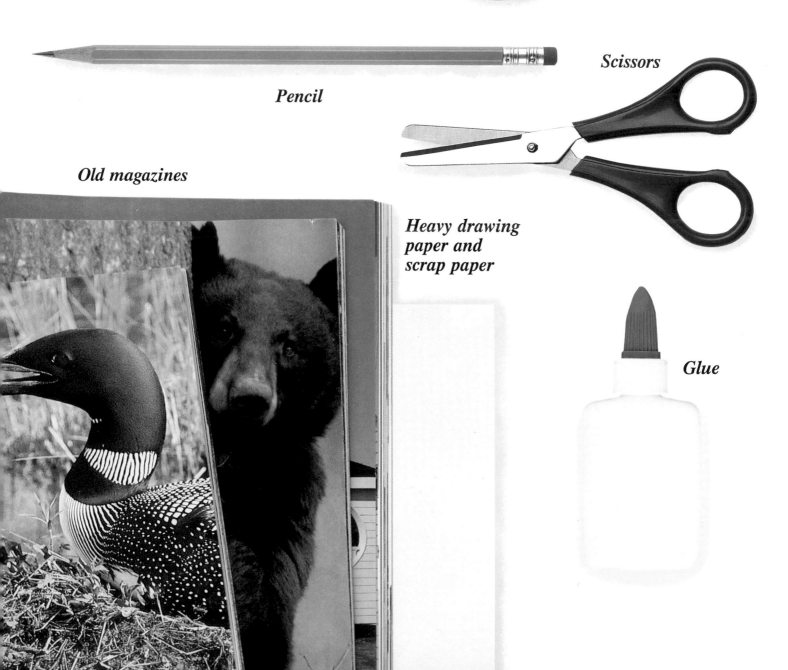

Cut photos out of old magazines and glue them on white paper. Draw light lines connecting them, being careful to make things the same size or *in proportion*.

Use tempera paints to color in the areas you've sketched. Mix the paint to match the colors in the photos. Test each color on scrap paper.

Watercolor Batik

Painting with Resists

Batik is the art of decorating cloth with *resist* designs. Part of the cloth is covered with wax or paste. The rest of the cloth is painted. The covered-up areas block out the paint—they resist being colored. After the paint has dried, the resist material is cleaned off and the uncolored cloth shines through.

Flour paste: (Ask an adult to help you.) Mix ½ cup white flour, ½ cup water, and 2 teaspoons alum (find alum where spices or medicines are sold). Using a blender works best—start with plain water, then slowly sprinkle in the flour and alum.

Watercolor paints

Materials needed:

Brushes

Day One

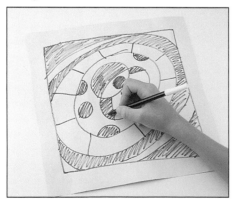

1 Plan your painting on scrap paper. Use your sketch as a guide when you "draw" with paste on the cloth.

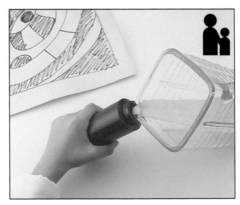

2 Mix up a batch of flour paste and pour it into an empty squeeze bottle (a plastic ketchup bottle or dish soap bottle is fine).

3 Squeeze the paste onto the cloth following your design. You'll make interesting drips and blobs. Let it dry overnight.

*9 × 12-inch (22 × 30 cm)
prewashed white cloth*

Squeeze bottle

Rinse water

Pencils and scrap paper

Day Two

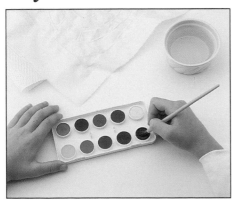

4 Place your cloth with its dried paste design on a pile of paper towels. Mix the colors you want for your painting.

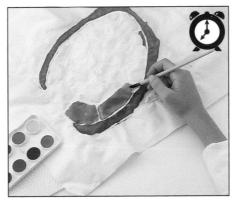

5 Paint the open areas of your cloth. The colors will look lighter as they dry, so use a lot of bright paint. Let it dry overnight.

Day Three

6 Work hard with your fingers to crack and rub the dried paste off the cloth. The strip of cloth beneath the paste resisted the color!

Finished Batiks

Ask a grown-up to help you iron the cloth if it's wrinkled. Abstract designs and simple picture batiks make beautiful works of art!

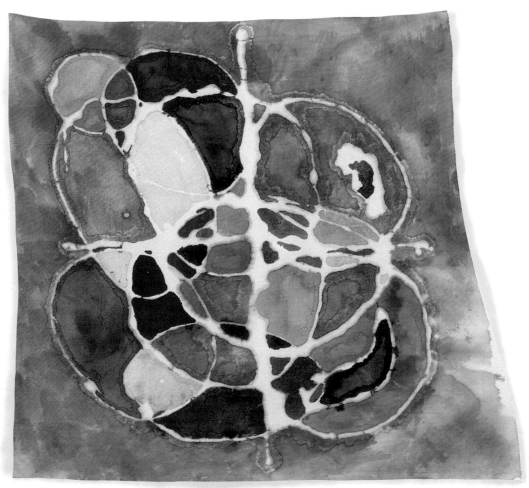

Batiks in Action

Shirt
Slip a pile of newspapers into a cotton T-shirt and batik the front. Use fabric paints so the colors won't wash out.

Pillow
Your batik can be made into a pillow with a bit of stitching and stuffing. Use fabric paints if you want your cloth to be washable.

Wall Hanging

Glue smooth dowels or natural twigs to the top and bottom edges of your batik. When the glue has dried, tie a string to the top stick for hanging.

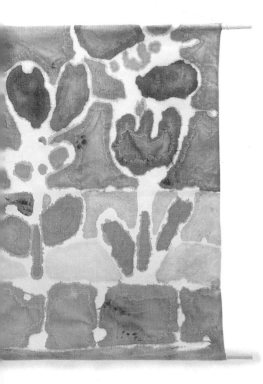

Resist Adventure

There are many other ways to experiment with resist painting. Here are two ways to try resist painting on paper instead of cloth. Any way you try it, it's fun to resist!

Crayon Resist

1 With a white crayon, draw a picture, message or abstract design on a piece of white paper.

2 Paint over your design with watercolors or tempera paint. The crayon resists being painted.

Glue Resist

1 Draw a design with white glue. Let it dry and then paint over it.

2 Use one color or a combination of beautiful colors. The glue resists the paint!

Paint Making

Making Paints and Pigments

Many years ago, artists had to make their own paints. You can make your own paint just because it's fun! Pretend you can't buy any ready-made paint. Experiment and invent different recipes and colors.

Materials needed:

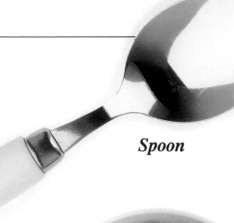

Spoon

Containers

Mixing bowl
Water

Colored chalk (or powdered drink mix)

1 Powdered colors are called pigments. Make your own pigments by grinding colored chalk with stones.

2 Crack two raw eggs into a bowl. Pour off the clear egg whites and save the yellow yolks.

3 Add a little bit of water and stir until you make a smooth, runny syrup. Pour it into several small containers.

Stones and paper plate

Vegetable oil

Pigments (bricks, dirt, or frozen berries)

Eggs

4 Add pigment to each dish to create the colors you want. Bright colors look the best—use powdered drink mix if you wish.

5 Paint with your egg tempera paint on heavy paper or cloth. Wash out the dishes before the egg mixture dries in them.

6 Don't stop with eggs! Ask for permission to paint with ketchup, mustard, orange juice, grape juice and more!

Prehistoric Paints

1 Pretend you're a caveman and collect samples of mud, dirt or pieces of brick. Look for lots of different colors.

2 Use stones to grind them into powder. For brighter colors, mash some frozen strawberries, blueberries or raspberries.

3 Mix oil with your pigments to make paints. Use a homemade brush and paint on a rock or piece of bark.